EDGE
BOOKS

INFECTED!

TUBERCULOSIS

HOW THE WHITE DEATH CHANGED HISTORY

by Mark L. Lewis

Consultant

Andrew DiNardo, MD
Assistant Professor of Global and Immigrant Health
Baylor College of Medicine

CAPSTONE PRESS
a capstone imprint

Edge Books are published by Capstone Press,
1710 Roe Crest Drive, North Mankato, Minnesota 56003
www.mycapstone.com

Library of Congress Cataloging-in-Publication Data
Names: Lewis, Mark L., 1991- author.
Title: Tuberculosis : how the white death changed history / Mark L. Lewis.
Description: North Mankato, Minnesota : Capstone Press, 2020 | Series:
  Infected! | Includes bibliographical references and index.
Identifiers: LCCN 2018061082 (print) | LCCN 2019000502 (ebook) | ISBN
  9781543572452 (ebook) | ISBN 9781543572414 (hardcover)
Subjects: LCSH: Tuberculosis—Juvenile literature. |
  Tuberculosis—History—Juvenile literature. |
  Tuberculosis—Treatment—Juvenile literature. | Diseases and
  history—Juvenile literature.
Classification: LCC RA644.T7 (ebook) | LCC RA644.T7 L4895 2020 (print) | DDC
  616.99/5--dc23
LC record available at https://lccn.loc.gov/2018061082

All internet sites appearing in back matter were available and accurate when this book was sent to press.

Editorial Credits
Editor: Megan Ellis
Designer: Craig Hinton
Production Specialist: Craig Hinton

Photo Credits
Alamy: Chronicle, 17, History and Art Collection, 20; AP Images: John Froschauer, 29, Rutgers University, 27; Getty Images: Mirrorpix, 22–23; iStockphoto: duncan1890, 19, Steve Debenport, 25, unoL, 21, zdravinjo, 14; Science Source: Arthur Glauberman, 14–15; Shutterstock Images: Brian A Jackson, 6–7, exzamp, 24, Kateryna Kon, cover (top), 1, Komsan Loonprom, cover (bottom), kwanchai.c, 10, Milosz Maslanka, 11, sladkozaponi, 5, Tatiana Shepeleva, 9, Ttatty, 12–13

Design Elements
Shutterstock Images

Printed in the United States of America.
PA70

TABLE OF CONTENTS

Chapter 1

A DRUG-RESISTANT DISEASE............4

Chapter 2

WHAT CAUSES TUBERCULOSIS?.........8

Chapter 3

THE HISTORY OF TUBERCULOSIS.......12

Chapter 4

MEDICAL ADVANCEMENTS...............18

Chapter 5

TREATING TUBERCULOSIS...............24

Glossary....................................30
Read More 31
Internet Sites............................31
Index 32

A DRUG-RESISTANT DISEASE

Patients filled the waiting room of a hospital in Mumbai, India. One of these patients was a 19-year-old engineering student. She had been on **antibiotics** for a lung infection for a year. But she wasn't getting better. She came to the hospital in Mumbai to get help.

Doctors diagnosed her with tuberculosis. Tuberculosis is also known as TB. It is a deadly disease that causes patients to cough. This spreads tuberculosis **bacteria**.

antibiotic—a medicine that targets bacteria
bacterium—a tiny organism that can cause illness

The tuberculosis bacteria were attached to the walls of the patient's lungs. She coughed and had a fever. However, the antibiotics that the doctors gave her weren't working. This version of tuberculosis was **drug-resistant**. Doctors gave her medicine without knowing if the drugs would help.

Many people live close together in Mumbai, India. This allows diseases to spread quickly.

drug-resistant—does not respond as effectively to medicine

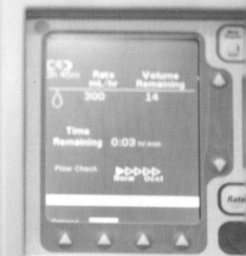

Some patients with drug-resistant TB need to take medications delivered through their veins.

300mL/H

TB is curable, but the disease spreads quickly without proper medical treatment. Doctors need to be sure that all bacteria are killed. If bacteria are left in the patient, the patient can become sick again and spread the illness to other people. Two million people in India contract tuberculosis every year. Of those people, 62,000 do not respond to typical treatments.

Doctors needed to find a new way to treat the woman in Mumbai. Medicine that cured TB no longer worked. The illness and medicine left the young woman thin and frail. Her **immune system** had a difficult time fighting the bacteria.

For many patients, the next step in treatment is a series of highly toxic drugs. It may include up to two years of **chemotherapy**. With careful treatment, patients can make a full recovery. But only about 50 percent of people with drug-resistant tuberculosis recover. TB kills approximately 1.6 million people every year.

immune system—the part of the body that fights infections
chemotherapy—a disease treatment that uses chemicals

CHAPTER 2

WHAT CAUSES TUBERCULOSIS?

The bacterium *Mycobacterium tuberculosis* causes TB infection. It travels through the air. When a person breathes in the bacteria, they attach to the person's lungs. Then the bacteria multiply and spread. TB can spread to other parts of the body such as the spine, brain, and kidneys. However, the most common area is the lungs.

DISEASE AND INFECTION

Most people do not get sick after inhaling tuberculosis bacteria. It is estimated that 25 percent of the world's population has been infected with tuberculosis bacteria.

FAST FACT

Some movies and books use the image of a person coughing blood into a white handkerchief to show that the person has TB.

Only 5 to 10 percent of people ever develop symptoms of TB disease. About 50 percent of those people develop symptoms within two years.

TB disease occurs when a person's immune system has trouble fighting the tuberculosis bacteria. This causes the person to get sick. The most common symptoms are fevers and night sweats. Many people also have a long-lasting cough. The coughing is the most visible symptom. People cough up blood without treatment. TB was very deadly before treatments became available.

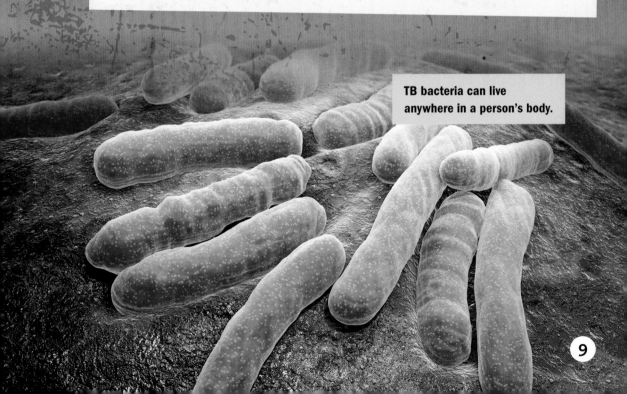

TB bacteria can live anywhere in a person's body.

People can cover their mouths with masks to help reduce the spread of certain diseases such as TB.

SPREADING THE DISEASE

People who do not show symptoms of TB typically do not spread the disease to others. Medical professionals refer to these as **latent** infections. They believe that these people have strong immune responses that fight the bacteria. This keeps them from getting sick.

latent—without symptoms

However, people showing symptoms of TB disease are more likely to pass the bacteria to others. When they cough, some bacteria leave their lungs. The bacteria become airborne. Other people inhale them. Not all of these people become sick. But TB bacteria can be hard to get rid of once they are in someone's lungs. TB disease can even show up later in life.

TB disease is mostly spread through the air. This is different from some other diseases such as cholera. People cannot catch TB by shaking a patient's hand. TB does not spread through water.

One sick person in a crowded place can pass TB to many people.

FAST FACT

Some very rare strains of TB spread through contaminated milk or meat products.

CHAPTER 3

THE HISTORY OF TUBERCULOSIS

Scientists believe that tuberculosis bacteria have been around for more than 15,000 years. The types of tuberculosis bacteria that exist today developed between 250 and 1,000 years ago.

FAST FACT

Tuberculosis is the leading cause of death from infectious diseases worldwide.

Scans of Egyptian mummies show evidence of TB bacteria in their spines. Some Egyptian art shows people who may have had complications from tuberculosis.

Hippocrates, an Ancient Greek physician, wrote about TB around the year 400 BC. However, people did not fully understand TB until recent years.

Tuberculosis has been found in ancient Egyptian mummies.

CONTAGIOUS OR NOT?

Girolamo Fracastoro, an Italian poet and physician, had a **hypothesis** about TB in 1546. He wrote that clothes and bedsheets could contain TB bacteria. He was one of the first people to suggest that TB disease was contagious. Most doctors at that time believed that tuberculosis was **hereditary**. They prescribed treatments such as drinking milk, eating butter that was boiled with honey, and exercising. They did not accept Fracastoro's hypothesis.

Doctors used to prescribe milk to cure tuberculosis. Patients did not get better by drinking milk.

hypothesis—an educated guess about the outcome of an experiment
hereditary—passed down from one generation to another

normal lung

FAST FACT

People who smoke tobacco are more likely to contract tuberculosis. This is because smoking damages a person's lungs.

smoker's lung

In 1720, an English physician named Benjamin Marten agreed with Fracastoro's hypothesis. Marten said that TB was caused by tiny living **organisms**. People could pass these organisms to one another. But doctors did not believe Marten either.

organism—a living thing

In the 1700s, most doctors believed that illnesses were caused by imbalances in the four humors. The theory stated that each person had four humors in his or her body: blood, phlegm, yellow bile, and black bile. When one of these became unbalanced, a person developed an illness. Curing the illness was a matter of putting the humors back in balance.

Doctors used a treatment called purging, which was making the patient vomit. They also used bloodletting, which included removing some of the patient's blood. These treatments existed as far back as ancient Greece and Rome. Unfortunately, they did not work. Cuts often became infected as a result of bloodletting. Both treatments weakened patients even more and made them sicker.

THE FOUR HUMORS

Doctors connected the four humors of the human body with the seasons. Each humor also had a corresponding element: earth, wind, water, and fire. Doctors thought that during certain seasons people received excess of one of the humors. For example, blood was associated with spring and air.

Bloodletting involved cutting open a patient's skin and removing blood.

CHAPTER 4

MEDICAL ADVANCEMENTS

TB has been around for hundreds of years. But it was not a widespread issue until the 1800s. Most TB outbreaks were small before then. They were often contained. In the 1800s, there were several TB **epidemics**. TB spread from Europe to North America. Because people did not know how to treat TB, many patients died. For example, one hospital in Paris, France, noted that in the early 1800s, more than one-third of the patients who died had TB.

POPULATION INCREASES

In the 1800s, many people moved from rural areas of Great Britain into cities. This was because of the Industrial Revolution. There were new factories and businesses in the cities.

epidemic—widespread outbreak of a disease

People wanted to find work in the cities. But cities quickly became crowded. There were not enough houses for all the people. Many people lived close together. The streets were dirty. By 1830, there was a thick **smog** in the air in London, England, and in other cities in Great Britain. TB spread quickly through the cities. But doctors did not know how to help patients.

Factories in England burned coal to power machines. This created pollution.

smog—dirty air; a combination of the words *smoke* and *fog*

A breakthrough came in 1865. Jean Antoine Villemin, a French scientist, proved that TB could spread from a human to an animal. Villemin injected fluids from a TB patient into a rabbit. Three months later, the rabbit developed TB symptoms. Villemin believed that this proved an organism caused TB.

Jean Antoine Villemin lived from 1827 to 1892.

FAST FACT

More than one-third of the people who died during the tuberculosis epidemic in England and Wales in the 1800s were between the ages of 15 and 34.

Villemin tested his theories about tuberculosis on rabbits. Some scientists today use rabbits and other animals to learn about diseases.

FAST FACT

Tuberculosis had many names in the 1800s, including the graveyard cough, the white death, and consumption.

Villemin's colleagues did not believe him. It took another 20 years before German scientist Robert Koch proved that bacteria caused TB.

SANATORIUMS

Robert Koch's findings helped cities understand how tuberculosis spread. In the late 1800s, people with TB were sent away to **sanatoriums**. The first sanatoriums were built in the Alps mountain range in Europe. The doctors relied on fresh air and open spaces as the primary treatments.

Some patients at sanatoriums slept outside.

sanatorium—a hospital for people with TB

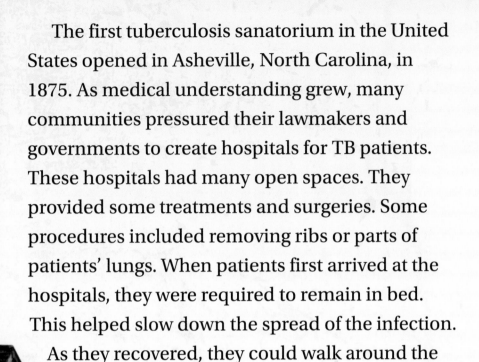

The first tuberculosis sanatorium in the United States opened in Asheville, North Carolina, in 1875. As medical understanding grew, many communities pressured their lawmakers and governments to create hospitals for TB patients. These hospitals had many open spaces. They provided some treatments and surgeries. Some procedures included removing ribs or parts of patients' lungs. When patients first arrived at the hospitals, they were required to remain in bed. This helped slow down the spread of the infection. As they recovered, they could walk around the sanatorium grounds.

CHAPTER 5

TREATING TUBERCULOSIS

Most sanatoriums closed soon after the end of World War II (1939–1945). As technology advanced and doctors developed antibiotics to treat tuberculosis, sanatoriums were no longer needed.

DEVELOPING A VACCINE

Two French scientists, Albert Calmette and Camille Guérin, created a TB vaccine in 1921. The **vaccine** took 13 years to finish.

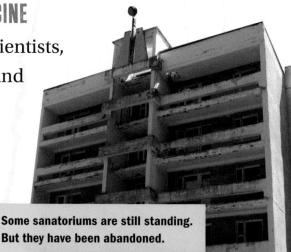

Some sanatoriums are still standing. But they have been abandoned.

vaccine—a substance made up of dead, weakened, or living organisms that is given to a person to protect against a disease

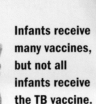

Infants receive many vaccines, but not all infants receive the TB vaccine.

The vaccine is given to infants in countries where TB is **endemic**. When infants receive the vaccine early, their bodies can fight the infection. The vaccine does not work for adults.

This vaccine is still used today. But it is only 80 percent effective. Scientists are working on improved vaccines and treatments.

endemic—regularly found in a certain area

FINDING A CURE

Selman Waksman was an American scientist. He and his colleagues discovered streptomycin in 1943. Streptomycin is an antibiotic. It comes from organisms that live in the soil.

Waksman found that streptomycin was an effective antibiotic against TB. Antibiotics kill bacteria that cause diseases. Waksman gave streptomycin to humans in 1949. These patients recovered from TB disease. However, some of them got TB again. TB had developed a resistance to streptomycin.

TUBERCULOSIS AND HIV/AIDS

In the mid-1980s there was a spike in the number of tuberculosis deaths in the United States. Deaths from TB in the United States rose from 22,201 in 1985 to 26,673 in 1992. This was caused in part by the human immunodeficiency virus (HIV). HIV is a virus that attacks cells in the body's immune system. Without anti-viral medicines, HIV attacks the immune system and causes acquired immunodeficiency syndrome (AIDS). Patients with AIDS have weak immune systems. They are easily infected by other diseases such as tuberculosis. Additionally, it is hard for their bodies to heal from TB.

In 1952, scientists created a cure known as triple therapy. Doctors across the world worked together. They tried many different medications. They found that TB returned when patients received only one medication. However, patients who received more than one medication recovered from TB disease. When doctors prescribed three antibiotics at the same time, also known as triple therapy, TB was less likely to come back. However, triple therapy treatment took a long time. Some patients used triple therapy for up to two years.

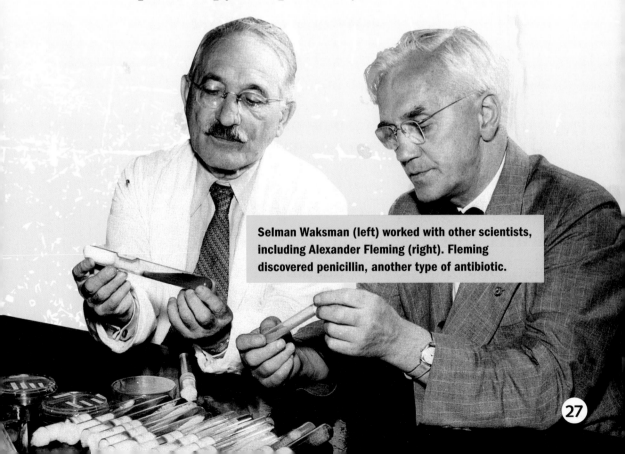

Selman Waksman (left) worked with other scientists, including Alexander Fleming (right). Fleming discovered penicillin, another type of antibiotic.

TUBERCULOSIS TODAY

Today doctors try to diagnose TB disease as early as possible. Doctors use skin or blood tests to find TB bacteria. If the test is positive, a doctor will order a chest x-ray or a **sputum** sample to see if the bacteria are active.

Curing tuberculosis still takes a long time. Doctors prescribe heavy doses of oral antibiotics. They use treatments similar to triple therapy. However, doctors use four antibiotics instead of three. This treatment lasts for at least six months. If the infection isn't completely gone, the patient must continue taking the antibiotics.

Doctors monitor their patients' symptoms and lab results. This helps doctors decide how long to continue antibiotics. If bacteria are left in a person's body, they can create more drug-resistant bacteria. That person could develop TB disease again. Doctors worry about epidemics when strains of drug-resistant TB spread. Drug-resistant TB is especially difficult to treat.

sputum—a mix of spit and mucus that is coughed up from the lungs

Tuberculosis affects millions of people every year. TB bacteria develop new resistances to drugs. Scientists continue to study the disease to better understand how to cure people who become infected.

FAST FACT

On an x-ray, tuberculosis disease looks like a person has cobwebs in his or her lungs.

Chest x-rays can help doctors diagnose problems with patients' lungs.

GLOSSARY

antibiotic (an-tih-bye-AW-tik)—a medicine that targets bacteria

bacterium (bak-TEER-ee-uhm)—a tiny organism that can cause illness

chemotherapy (key-moh-THARE-uh-pee)—a disease treatment that uses chemicals

drug-resistant (DRUG ruh-SIS-tant)—does not respond as effectively to medicine

endemic (en-DEH-mik)—regularly found in a certain area

epidemic (eh-pih-DEH-mik)—widespread outbreak of a disease

hereditary (huh-REH-dih-teh-ree)—passed down from one generation to another

hypothesis (hi-PAH-thuh-sis)—an educated guess about the outcome of an experiment

immune system (ih-MEWN SIS-tem)—the part of the body that fights infections

latent (LAY-tent)—without symptoms

organism (OR-gah-ni-sum)—a living thing

sanatorium (san-uh-TOR-ee-um)—a hospital for people with TB

smog (SMOG)—dirty air; a combination of the words *smoke* and *fog*

sputum (SPEW-tuhm)—a mix of spit and mucus that is coughed up from the lungs

vaccine (vak-SEEN)—a substance made up of dead, weakened, or living organisms that is given to a person to protect against a disease

READ MORE

Cummings, Judy Dodge. *Epidemics and Pandemics: Real Tales of Deadly Diseases.* Mystery & Mayhem. White River Junction, Vt.: Nomad Press, 2018.

Klepeis, Alicia Z. *Bizarre Things We've Called Medicine.* History of the Bizarre. North Mankato, Minn.: Capstone Press, 2016.

Mould, Steve. *The Bacteria Book: The Big World of Really Tiny Microbes.* New York: DK, 2018.

INTERNET SITES

CDC: Tuberculosis: Personal Stories
https://www.cdc.gov/tb/default.htm

KidsHealth: Tuberculosis
https://kidshealth.org/en/parents/tuberculosis.html

Women's and Children's Health Network: The Immune System
https://www.cyh.com/HealthTopics/HealthTopicDetailsKids.aspx?p=335&np=152&id=2402

INDEX

acquired immunodeficiency syndrome (AIDS), 26
antibiotics, 4, 5, 24, 26, 27, 28

bacteria, 4, 5, 7, 8, 9, 10, 11, 12, 14, 21, 26, 28, 29
bloodletting, 16

Calmette, Albert, 24
chemotherapy, 7

Fracastoro, Girolamo, 14, 15

Great Britain, 18–19
Guerin, Camille, 24

Hippocrates, 13
human immunodeficiency virus (HIV), 26
humors, 16

India, 4, 7
Industrial Revolution, 18–19

Koch, Robert, 21, 22

lungs, 4, 5, 8, 11, 15, 23

Marten, Benjamin, 15
mummies, 12

purging, 16

sanatoriums, 22–23, 24
streptomycin, 26

triple therapy, 27, 28

vaccines, 24–25
Villemin, Jean Antoine, 20–21

Waksman, Selman, 26
World War II, 24, 25

x-rays, 28